Ken + Tina,

Enjoy + Share

David H. Scott

THE GENERAL'S DRIVER
A VIETNAM SOLDIER REMEMBERS

BY DAVID H. SCOTT

OCTOBER 1966 TO OCTOBER 1968

B 2ND 502 101ST AIRBORNE

LT. GENERAL ROSSON'S DRIVER AND PERSONAL AIDE

LT. GENERAL STILWILL'S PERSONAL AIDE

CONTENTS

FOREWORD

I suppose at some time we all consider writing a book on something extraordinary that happened in our lives and upon hearing one's story, someone is always saying, "You should write a book about that." I decided after fifty years to do just that.

This book started out as nothing more than what I was calling a "narrative." I believe and hope it has turned out to be a little bit more than that.

It was written mainly for my children, members of my family and what few friends I have left alive. There is nothing more at issue here than to give its readers an idea of this soldier's experiences in Vietnam.

I have not forgotten the few men I knew. The faces I remember; the names on the "Wall." I cherish those relationships, those memories both good and bad. They have stayed with me every minute of every day since I left Vietnam.

If it wasn't for the ultimate sacrifice that some of those great men gave, I would not be here today to tell my small part in what an experience it was, to say the least.

May God Bless those men.

DEDICATION

**This book is dedicated to S/MSGT Bennie L. Dexter
Captured on May 10, 1966**

Case 0333

On May 10, 1966, Airman 2nd Class Bennie Lee Dexter was captured by communist forces while driving a jeep south on National Route 14 near the Darlac/Quang Duc Province border, South Vietnam. His jeep was found at this location the next day and there was a Vietnamese witness to his capture. Subsequent intelligence reports confirmed Bennie Dexter's capture and named the location at which he was being held. Bennie Dexter was placed in Prisoner of War status.

Bennie Dexter was born on July 18, 1944. He was part of the Bend Senior High School Class of 1964, in Bend, Oregon finishing his high school diploma requirements in the Air Force. Bennie entered the Air Force on September 25, 1963 and was stationed at Lackland Air Force Base for basic training. He then graduated from the 3320th technical school at Amarillo Air Force Base, Texas, on February 10, 1964 and was assigned for Lajes Field, Azores, Portugal in March 1964. Bennie received orders for Vietnam and arrived at 6251 CS Gp, Bien Hoa AB, RVN (PACAF), 4 October 1965, coincidently on my 18th Birthday. His unit was then sent to Pleiku, RVN (Republic of Vietnam) in April 1966 as part of the 7th AF / 633rd Combat Support Group / 3rd Support Squadron.

There is no information as to why Bernie was driving on that specific highway and what he was doing. During the entire time until he was declared "administratively deceased" he was listed as a POW. As recently as March of 2016 there was an area excavated to try to find Bennie's remains at a location that was a possible burial site.

One can go to this YouTube link and view the video of the excavation of the site: **www.youtube.com/watch?v=2lqEwsgwkN4.**

In the limited intelligence and documentation there is an account:

An excavation of the area was conducted with negative results.

There is no definitive proof this is what happened. As late as 1974 there is documentation from the Department of Defense that "Bennie' was reportedly held in 1974 at a location in Phuoc Ninh District, Tay Ninh Province in South Vietnam.

More troubling is the fact that during Testimony given by a high raking Czech General Jan Sejna, the highest Communist official ever to defect to the west, is the fact that numerous, dozens of Vietnam War POW's were transferred from POW Camps in both South Vietnam and North Vietnam to the Soviet Union via Czechoslovakia. This took place in the beginning of 1966, another group in 1966 and spring of 1967. All three groups consisted roughly of twenty to twenty-five American POW's.

You will never be forgotten Bennie Dexter.

DECEMBER 14, 2017 THURSDAY EVENING
A LETTER I WROTE TO MYSELF

I just finished watching the PBS ten-part series *The Vietnam War* a film by Ken Burns and Lynn Novick.

I also just completed and sent off to my editor and publisher at the same time the 4th editing of the book: *The General's Driver, A Vietnam Soldier Remembers.* The book is about my twenty-six months in Vietnam, to include the first year in Vietnam with the 101st Airborne.

For weeks I have been watching the series and working on the book. I wish I would have neither started the book nor watched the series. I am not sure watching the series was a smart thing for me to do. Just like I have never gotten the courage to go back to Washington D.C. and view the "Wall" and spend some time. I probably should. Just to get it over with.

By writing the book and watching the series, it obviously has brought back a lot of feelings and memories I have worked hard at suppressing and trying to keep hidden. Perhaps it will turn out it is a good thing that I finally took the time and told some of my experiences in Vietnam during those twenty-six months.

I am depressed as I haven't been for quite some time. I am angry, disgusted, feel hollow, feel unworthy, feel isolated and feel terribly alone.

I don't know who to talk to. I don't know who to reach out to. I just don't know what to do. I am having a hard time trying to under-stand why at this stage in my life I must go through this again. Why I must face this alone and have no one to lean on or help me through it.

Am I suicidal? I think so. Not the 1st time to be sure. I am tired and somewhat fed up. I am very lonely at this time in my life. But I have dealt with these kinds of feelings for fifty years now and it doesn't leave me. I am about as unmotivated and outright immobilized as I can ever remember being for a long, long time.

CHAPTER 1

I MIGHT HAVE TO CARRY YOU

I am not going to get into the controversy of the Vietnam war.

The United States lost that war. Plain and simple.

In the first action I saw I was part of two squads. Maybe three. Lieutenant Belding was with us—he was our platoon leader. He wouldn't have been with us if I had been part of a lone squad.

Each squad was comprised of seven to nine soldiers. One guy carried an M-60 machine gun; a couple of guys carried ammo for him. One guy had an M-79 grenade launcher. Another guy normally had a 30-06 with a scope. The rest of us had our M-16s. A few of us had a Claymore mine in our packs.

We had a M-60 mortar with us—it took several of us to carry the three pieces. Some of us were also carrying mortar rounds in our packs, one each.

It didn't take me long to figure out that the most important thing I could take in my pack and on my ammo belt was as much ammo as I could carry. I carried twice as much as some of the other guys—I could never have too much ammo. More than likely, no matter how much I had, it wasn't going to be enough. Besides, somebody was always running out of ammo.

I grew up around guns. My father was an avid hunter and had many guns. I was shooting rifles and shotguns at a very early age. I was very comfortable with my capabilities.

I wasn't one for spraying the bushes and the trees with bullets helter-skelter. I believed in taking aim and shooting at what you could see—and hitting it, if you were patient. There was luck to it also, but just shooting for the sake of shooting never made sense to me.

We had been out several days, and we were on our way up an incline. It was not steep; tall pine-like trees, open ground, not a lot of brush—certainly wasn't jungle terrain. I was second in line. The guy on point and I alternated all the time. I always tried to be the guy behind him. I enjoyed point. The point man saw somebody next to a tree and took a shot at him with his M-79. This guy liked point like I did, and he liked the M-79 because he was good with it and had determined he could cover a larger area with the M-79 round than he could with a few rounds of an M-16.

When we got to where the point man had seen the shadowy figure, we saw the body lying behind the tree. He had killed an enemy soldier. He had just lobbed that round next to the tree, slightly beyond it.

I heard our guys coming up behind us. Then all hell broke loose. We had walked into an ambush. The Viet Cong were in front of us and on both sides. You can't mistake the sound of an AK-47 round whizzing by your head or through the trees and bushes. The enemy soldiers were no different than us. They were just spraying the area with as many bullets as they could shoot. Things were happening so fast and we were moving so quickly to the front, left and right that nobody was paying attention to our rear. In seconds they could fill in behind us. If that were to happen as I remember it vividly, we were going to be in trouble.

I was trained to immediately drop my pack, get in a horizontal line with the other soldiers and start firing aggressively with overwhelming firepower, moving forward with no hesitation. That is what we did; it was kind of like moving in a box formation, some guys got in line and went forward. Some of the guys got in line and went to the left. The rest of the guys got in line and went to the right.

Nobody covered our backs because we got caught up in the moment, trying to keep the enemy busy and from maneuvering behind us. The danger of getting caught up in the moment and moving fast in all three forward directions was you could stray too far from each other. Each line of soldiers ran the risk of getting surrounded by the enemy coming in behind them. It didn't take long in a fire fight to get too far, real fast.

The lieutenant decided that it would be wise for us to form up and get into a defensive perimeter. Night was coming on—the last thing we needed was to be strung out at dark. When the shooting died down, the lieutenant called in a couple of gunships to harass our perimeter. It didn't take long for the enemy to hunker down or disperse. Of course, the enemy knew where he was dispersing to.

As we started to form up and create a circle, I decided to head back down the hill to get my pack and any other packs I could find and carry. I knew an M-60 mortar round was in my pack—we had the mortar but no rounds. I went down the hill and for the life of me I couldn't find even one pack, let alone mine. It was scary. Here I was out by of the perimeter by myself. I felt completely out of sorts because I just couldn't believe we had come that far up the hill. I kept looking and looking, going further and further down the hill. I never did find any of the packs. I was lucky just to get back up the hill to the guys and not get caught out in the open by the enemy, alone, way down the hill where we had come from. The only thing that I imagined could have happened is that, once we dropped the packs and got in line and headed up the hill shooting, the enemy came in behind us and grabbed those packs. They were waiting for us to drop them.

As darkness set in we took stock of our predicament: limited ammo, limited water, no food. Everything was in our packs. Dumbest thing I had ever been involved in up to that point. I vowed to myself and anybody else that would listen and I would never drop my pack again. If I were ordered to I would refuse.

There were still about an hour of daylight left, so I traded weapons with the guy who had the 30-06 with a scope. He took my M-16. Shooting an M-16 was a waste of ammo because you couldn't really see the enemy, even though now and then you could see them moving around from position to position, trying to getter a better shot at us.

If I am not mistaken, 50,000 rounds of ammunition were expended during the Vietnam War to kill one enemy combatant. That is a lot of ammunition going somewhere for no good.

We were almost at the crest of the hill, so the Viet Cong had to shoot uphill. We were all prone on the ground, behind upright trees or trees that were down. We certainly weren't well concealed. As the afternoon progressed, several guys got shot through the butt because sometimes your butt was higher than your head. Now we had one killed and five wounded, one of the five was shot in the gut. His name was Singleton—he died after he was taken out the next morning.

From my position I had a good view of three enemy soldiers hiding behind a downed tree down the hill. I believed I had a better chance of getting them with the 30-06 and the scope. I worked patiently on picking them off, one by one.

There was nothing we could do for our wounded comrades. The medic did the best he could. It was nearly dark.

Lt. Belding came to me and said: "We need to get these wounded soldiers medivaced out 1st thing in the morning. Scott, I want you and two other guys to clear a small area down to the left in the morning, so we can have a chopper come in at the break of day." "Yes sir" is all I said, knowing it was up to me to pick the other two guys to go with me.

Two of the other guys said they would go with me in my squad. Whilhimie and Hudgens both didn't hesitate at all. Hudgens said: "Whilhimie and me will be ready to go thirty minutes before daylight." What this meant was we would have to go out of the perimeter to clear the area, just the three of us. All we could hope for was that none of the enemy soldiers were in that area. Lt. Belding once again came to me and said: "Scott I am going to call for the chopper now, so you have to have that area cleared for them to land by one hour after daylight." Once again all I said was "yes sir."

Then Lt. Belding said: "Once you get them on the chopper, then we all will head up to the crest of the hill and clear a large enough LZ for three choppers to land at one time for resupply." The resupply meant new packs, food, everything. The lieutenant made a list of essentials and radioed it back to the company commander, who assured us that he would get it to us by 10 A.M.

As I looked around five guys in the platoon were wounded. One was dead. The wounded were inside the perimeter with us. The dead one was down the hill. We could see him lying there. It was a tense situation. The only thing the lieutenant could think of was to call back the gunships and have them stick with us all night long, which is what they did. The gunships traded off every two hours or so throughout the night

It was a long night—the longest night until then that I was forced to spend in the field. Once it got dark Lieutenant Belding and I went out of the perimeter and carried the dead soldier back in. He was a big guy and very heavy. My first experience of many in the coming year of carrying "dead weight."

I will never forget it. One of the smaller black guys whose name was Maverick took off pretty much all his clothes about 10 P.M. and snuck out of the perimeter. He spent a good two or three hours out roaming around. The guys told me he did it all the time. He counted the enemy dead. If he found one still alive he killed him with his knife. He was nuts. But he certainly wasn't a coward.

The three of us had managed to get a big enough landing zone cleared about 7 A.M. the next morning and the medivac chopper was right on time.

Then we all went to the top of the hill and started to clear an LZ for the three choppers that were due by 10 A.M. They also were right on time. We took most of the rest of the day to get our stuff packed and get squared away. Late that afternoon we took off again on patrol for several days.

Another incident I remember is one of the guys who wasn't very big was having a tough time keeping up. I remember him being red-headed and very thin. How he made it through jump school I just couldn't figure out. Some of the guys had no sympathy for him, none whatsoever. When he struggled, they threatened to leave him behind. I don't know if the lieutenant ever heard them or not, but this one time he was really struggling.

I took his pack and carried both his and mine for a long time, until he could get some of his strength back. He kept his M-16 and ammo belt, but of course relieved of a fifty-pound pack helped him immensely. Some of the guys didn't think it was the right thing to do.

I politely reminded them that one day I might have to carry theirs because they had gotten shot. "I might even have to carry you," I said. "You want that or want me to leave you behind?"

Nobody said anything after that. I took no shit from anybody, ever. I always stood my ground and I always was in their face, aggressive but with respect.

The first few months went on like this, out in the field for days then back in for days. When we were back in, we got things cleaned up, starting with ourselves. We kept the base area clean and waited until we were told to get ready to get picked up again by the helicopters.

CHAPTER 2

WHY I ENLISTED

All I remember is that she was cute. But then after a couple of beers or, in those days more than likely a couple of six-packs, the cute part didn't matter. I knew it was against the University of Oregon's Code of Conduct to be in a girl's dorm for any reason—especially to spend the night. What choice did I have? She was cute.

I thought I had sneaked out of her room unnoticed before daylight. My dorm room was right next door to her building. Evidently, I didn't sneak very well, because it was only a matter of hours and I was called before the Dean of Boys. I had been there before, standing in front of his desk. The guy didn't like me. I didn't care much for him either. I just couldn't understand why he had such a problem with me drinking beer, when and where I wanted to. Spending the night in a girl's dorm was a completely different matter. I knew I had broken a cardinal rule.

I tried to convince him he had the wrong guy—there were 5,000 other guys on campus, for God's sake.

"Yes, David, it is true there are 5,000 other guys on campus," he said, not a hint of humor in his voice or empathy on his lips. "But only one David H. Scott." "If it takes me the rest of the school year I am going to see that David H. Scott gets kicked out of the University of Oregon."

I had already received—or I should say my parents had received—several written reprimands concerning my unabashed use of alcohol, when and where I wanted. There was also something mentioned in one of the letters, if I remember correctly, about my harboring some kind of anti-social behavior.

I wasn't really getting anywhere at the university anyway. Things just weren't clicking on the learning side of things. But things sure were clicking well on the fun side of things.

About this time a good friend of mine by the name of Roy Buell from San Francisco committed suicide on a beach near San Francisco. He killed himself with a shotgun. I think his father was chief executive or chief financial officer for Ma Bell or Pac Bell or one of the "Big Bells" in those days. I had a tough time understanding his suicide and dealing with it. Roy and I had spent a lot of time together; I didn't see it coming.

Forty years later, Matt Boyd, my daughter Chrissi's ex-husband, shot himself in Redmond, Oregon. I was with Matt on a Sunday and the next Tuesday morning he decided to end it. I didn't see that coming either. Maybe if I had spent more time being a friend instead of being focused on myself so much, I could have done something.

When I left the Dean of Boys office in Eugene on that day in 1966, I decided that at this point in my life a college degree wasn't in the cards.

I called my Dad in Bend. He came over the Cascade Mountains and picked me up. He drove me to Portland to the Army recruiters office and I enlisted in the U. S. Army, Airborne Infantry. In 1966 that was going to lead me only one place: Vietnam.

I was on a bus immediately to Fort Ord, California to begin my Army Infantry training.

CHAPTER 3

BALLS THE SIZE OF GRAPEFRUITS

It didn't take me long to realize—once I got through the initial indoctrination, got my hair cut, collected my uniforms and gear— that I wasn't going to have that much of a problem getting into this training thing. If I could just learn to keep my mouth shut.

The drill instructors were tough, but always seemed to have a compassionate side to them. They were aggressive, in-your-face kind of guys. They were in superb physical shape. They didn't take shit from anybody. But for the most part I liked them all and got along with them.

What they were looking for were a few leaders; the rest would be the followers. From my first week, I quickly figured out that it was in my best interest to keep in tip-top shape, keep my uniforms starched and pressed, my shoes shined and my bunk area immaculate. I would show respect and equally important, help those who were struggling.

I learned in high school that a lot of guys gravitated toward me—not for all the right reasons, mind you. However, I was adventurous. I always wanted to be doing something, going somewhere, creating something and getting something going. Above all I wanted to have fun.

My mother instilled in me a sense of organization and cleanliness. I was a good cook. I washed the dishes. I kept my bedroom clean. I helped where I could and was orderly.

These attributes learned at an early age were now serving me well. The drill instructors, the platoon sergeant and the company commander all noticed. I was the kind of guy they were looking for. They were looking for someone who fully understood responsibility to help lead the men during training. They needed someone to hold accountable for the actions of the men—no different than when training would be over, and we would leave training to do the real thing. There were squad leaders, platoon sergeants, 1st sergeants, master sergeants, platoon 1st and 2nd lieutenants and company commanders who were Captains.

It didn't take too long before I was a squad leader. Then I was a platoon sergeant and then I was the company sergeant when I was in advanced infantry training (AIT) at Fort Gordon. But I am getting ahead of myself.

The biggest thing I realized during my first month of basic training was that I was liked by the other guys in training. They looked for leadership. I knew the Black guys liked me because I looked out for them, respected them, never insulted them and treated them as equals.

Getting ready for shipment to Vietnam, you trained as a unit. Then, when the training was complete you shipped over to Vietnam as a unit. The training wasn't that long because they needed fresh soldiers quickly. The Vietnam War was escalating.

It didn't work that way for me. During maneuvers, out in the field for several weeks, I contracted poison oak. It attacked me viciously. My testicles swelled up to the size of grapefruits. The only way I could move was hobbling around on crutches. The poison oak virus; hit me so hard that the medics furloughed me and sent me home to recuperate. I climbed into a Trailways bus at Carlsbad, California, destination Bend, Oregon.

The recuperation took several weeks. I took a bus back. All the guys I had gotten to know were already done with basic and were on to advanced infantry training (AIT). I got put in with a new bunch of guys. It didn't take me long—once again I was squad leader.

We finished basic training and we were shipped to Fort Gordon near Augusta, Georgia for AIT.

I don't remember a whole lot about this time, what we did, what was advanced about the training. As infantry soldiers in training, the training basically centered around how to keep your weapon clean, getting in shape, learning to take orders and follow those orders. It also included figuring out who could shoot and hit something and who couldn't. I was a good shot—that wasn't a problem for me.

At AIT I became a company sergeant and began wearing an arm band designating me as such. This didn't mean much, except when someone else did something wrong I got held accountable. Then when they did something right they alone got acknowledged for it. The armband did have its privileges: I never had to do KP. I never had to clean the toilets. I got my own room at the head of the bar-racks. With the door shut to my room, it served as the place the Black guys and I played poker and threw the dice.

I learned to be the first one up and the last one to bed. I learned to help the guys tackle something they strug-gled with. It became apparent to me I was one of the lucky ones who got respect. That made things a whole lot easier. Except—I had a hard time staying out of trouble when we got time off and went to town. A very hard time.

I remember this tall Black soldier named Williams. We hit it off. We really got along. The first time we went to town, we got thrown in jail. I don't remember for what exactly, but I am sure alcohol was involved. The captain of the company—I don't remember what his name was—came down and got us out of jail. I don't remember any ramifi-cations for that incident, although there had to have been something. But, let's face it: we weren't the first two soldiers in training to get thrown in jail in Macon, Georgia! Nor were we the first white man and black man to get thrown in jail together. At least I didn't lose my armband.

The second time it happened, things didn't go so well. This time I was by myself. Again, I can't remember the exact circumstances, but you can use your imagination. You probably wouldn't be too far off. The police left me in the drunk tank for an unusual amount of time. I am pretty sure it had something to do with that "anti-social attitude" some-one once accused me of displaying. This did not go over well, especially during the late 1960s in the heart of Georgia. A white guy from the West Coast, a smart- ass white guy at that, drunk in jail in a black drunk tank—an illuminating experience, to say the least.

To make matters worse, the captain took his time in coming to get me this time. Like two days. I can tell you that I didn't smell or look like a platoon sergeant—in or out of training—when he threw my sorry ass in the Jeep.

"Master sergeant is waiting to see you," he said. Not another peep on the half-hour ride back to base.

Now this master sergeant was the biggest, toughest black dude you ever saw in your life. I thought he liked me personally, but I wasn't sure that was going to do me any good. It didn't. He took me out back behind a tree trunk wide enough that nobody could see us. He told me to stand at attention.

"Scott, you ever get arrested again for any reason—whether you are under my command in training or you're out of training—and you fuck up like this again," he said. "I will beat the living shit out of you. I will hurt you ba-a-a-d."

He also told me that I was respected by all the guys, especially the Black guys because of the way I treated them.

"Where they are going, they'll need you," he said. "Most guys don't have a clue how to treat privates—black or white." I was, he said, a natural born leader. I was able to help them get through the hell that was coming. Getting thrown in jail was not setting a good example.

He could have taken my armband from me. But he didn't. I remained the company sergeant in training. I never screwed up again, at least there.

After AIT, we immediately went to Fort Benning, also in Georgia, for airborne training. Fort Benning is where the Army's jump school is.

Jump school lasted three weeks. To become certified as an Airborne soldier you had to jump out of an airplane five times. The first time I hesitated. The door man, who happened to be another big, Black master sergeant, kicked my ass out the door without saying a word. After that, I was always the first guy out the door.

When jump school was over, there was a commercial airline strike on. We couldn't get plane tickets to go home on our thirty day leave. Six of us pooled our money, bought an old car and drove across country, letting the first guy off at his house in the middle of the country. I was the next-to-last dropped off in Bend, and the last guy drove home to Seattle. That trip was the first time I saw the Grand Canyon. The first time I heard a mountain lion cry in the desert. It was the first time I realized I had friends I could count on.

Most of those friends never came home.

CHAPTER 4

STAYING ALIVE

We all knew when we went home for those thirty days of leave after graduating from jump school that we were going to Vietnam. It wasn't a matter of if. My orders told me to report to Travis Air Base out of San Francisco.

Once you reported in at Travis, they loaded us up in buses and took us to some large warehouse-type buildings in downtown San Francisco on the wharf. We were to spend a couple of days there until everyone else showed up and we were all together. Those of us who showed up early used the time to hoot and holler in the City by the Bay.

It was not easy to focus on having fun. The fact that we all had just left home after a thirty day leave was very stressful and created a type of anxiety that none of us had ever experienced before. The stress of just completing training, the news of the war escalating made it very hard to forget what we were heading in to, but for a guy who had a lot of practice at having fun, I managed to contribute my fair share those few days in San Francisco.

When the party was over, we found ourselves back on the buses and taken to the airbase. We got on large military-type transport aircraft heading across the Pacific for Southeast Asia. I don't remember where we stopped to refuel or how long it was when we stopped, but I do remember it was an awfully long flight. We were in our jungle fatigues, with our M-16 and some gear sitting in row after row of seats that were the most uncomfortable I had ever experienced.

Tan Son Nhut out of Saigon was the airfield where almost everyone going to or returning to and leaving Vietnam went before their assigned destination. I don't remember much about arriving. Many soldiers later described how hot and humid it was, or how much it was raining the first couple of weeks, or the smell of the place. None of that resonates with me now. I was there—the place where I knew I was going to end up when I joined the army.

What I do recall is that I was "culled" out of my company and assigned as a company clerk. I was shocked and extremely unhappy. There was no question why it happened. The Army wanted the guys who were sharp, on the ball and had initiative in the rear. I'm not trying to sound conceited—it is just a fact. Plus, I knew how to type, well and fast. That is the way it has always been. In World War II approximately 3 million soldiers served, but only about 750,000 were in combat. I am close to my numbers. During the Second World War it took three to four soldiers in the rear to support one in combat. In Vietnam only 20% of the soldiers serving in the country were in combat.

I was very upset. All the other guys I had trained with for the last four to five months were assigned to the B 2nd 502 101st Airborne. I believe that was Phang Rhang where the 101ˢᵗ headquarters was.

I was mad and angry. I let everyone know it. That didn't do me much good. My superiors kept reminding me I was in the Army. As a private I was expected to accept my orders, follow those orders and do what was needed to be done.

One morning without permission I knocked on the commander's door which was open. The commander said "Come In." "Sir, I was mistakenly assigned to your company. I am not a clerk or a typist. I have been trained as an infantry rifleman and I need to get to the men I trained with. Can you help me? I am requesting a transfer to the 101ˢᵗ." Then he looked at me puzzled and said "Are you nuts? You stay here you don't have to go out into combat!" It took a lot of persuasion, but he finally relented and in about a week I had new orders. I was transferred and hitched a ride aboard a C-130 to the B 2ⁿᵈ 502 101ˢᵗ Airborne.

When I arrived, the guys were not surprised to see me. On the day I arrived not all the guys I knew were out in the field. The company captain assigned me to a squad in a platoon that was due back in camp in a couple of days. Everyone in that squad were guys I knew and had trained with.

Again, I don't remember all the details, but it was the B 2ⁿᵈ 502 101ˢᵗ. Some Vietnam Vets can rattle off these kinds of details like it was yesterday. I just didn't keep that kind of information in my head. Same thing as to where I was in country. I do remember some places when I hear the names or read them. I have talked with some Vietnam Vets who can spit out every single place they were in Vietnam, why they were there, the day and the year, the battles they were in.

Not me. I just lived it and moved on. Here's the weird thing: there are events and places in Vietnam I remember vividly. I could get on a plane today, get in a vehicle and take you to the exact spot.

It was pretty much the same thing as my life progressed after I returned. I never remembered birthdays, anniversaries, what I did ten years ago on that given day, in that week, in that month or year.

My wife Debbie remembers everything: Her entire family tree, things we did years ago, the exact dates for all events. What the kids did and where they did it. It amazes me.

Remembering these sorts of experiences just was not important to me. Maybe it was because I was detached somewhat, above it, lived more for the moment. I was paying attention to that minute, that hour, that day—just keeping my head down and striving to staying alive.

CHAPTER 5

INTO THE FIELD

I went out into the field almost immediately, which is what it was called when you went on a mission. We got picked up by helicopters and taken to an LZ, Landing Zone, and dropped off. We then spent several days out on patrol. I didn't know it then, but it became common knowledge throughout the entire war that the Viet Cong and the North Vietnamese Army normally dictated when there would be an encounter with us. It could be a quick-fire fight; an ambush; it could be a battle that lasted hours or even days and sometimes weeks. But most of the time the enemy dictated the terms of whatever action took place, where it took place and for how long it lasted.

Things never really changed much from one week to the next. We were either in the rear at a base camp or we were in the field. We didn't engage the enemy as often as we would have liked. That is because, as I have said most of the time the engagements were on their terms.

This one time we were out in the field we were in hilly and rocky terrain. You might envision Vietnam as all jungle—not so.

We had been out for longer than usual. The guys in the rear were calling the shots, probably holding out and hoping we would run into something. You never really knew what everyone else was doing. Sometimes when you were not in the field and ran into someone who was present in a firefight or battle, you could trust what he was telling you. So, when you were out—unless another squad, platoon or company in your sphere of influence was in the thick of it— you had no clue what was going on.

We got orders to go help a sister company that was in a potential hostile situation. They might need some help. They were not that far away. The quickest way to get to them was up a sharp rocky hill; it wasn't really a mountain. On the way up and over I slipped and fell and hit my right elbow on a sharp rock. Keep in mind we were carrying our packs and our weapons. I just kept going and wrapped it up.

That night in the perimeter my elbow really started to bother me. Since it was dark, I couldn't turn on a light, so it got no attention. The next morning, I went to the medic. "Doc something isn't right. My arm is very sore; I am having trouble moving it. You need to look at it." "Take your shirt off" he said. After looking at it he said to me, "All I can do is lance the area that is swollen and full of puss. I will give you some antibiotics and wrap it up." With that done, we were off again to the other company.

When we met up with the other company and it was determined by Lt. Belding and the other Platoon Lieutenant there was no emergency… I knew I had a problem with my arm. It had gotten so swollen up I couldn't move my fingers and couldn't pull the trigger on my weapon. My pack was killing me. I found the Doc. "Doc this had gotten much worse. I can't move my fingers and can't pull the trigger on my weapon. Something is not right." "Take your shirt off," he said again. "Oh Boy" was all he said. He showed me the red streaks going up my arm to my neck area, down my chest and basically all over my upper body. He said: "you have a very serious blood poisoning situation. We need to get you out of here. I can't do anything for you."

The lieutenant and the medic decided to call in a medivac chopper to fly me out. I was obviously sick and down, but at the time didn't think much about the decision for that to happen. Other than medivacs for wounded and KIAs, we never had this happen before. I didn't feel bad because I was legitimately hurt—it wasn't like I had shot myself in the foot. I had huge misgivings about getting medivaced out and leaving my guys.

Once the chopper got there and a couple of the guys helped me on, I just laid down on the floor. The fact that I obviously didn't feel well plus the overwhelming relief of just getting out of the field hit me. I had a bit of an instant breakdown. As I remember it, I cried a lot. It was like my life just went out of me all at once as the chopper was lifting off the ground. No one saw it, but the door gunners and they saw this sort of thing every day and much worse.

Once back safely behind lines, I headed for the hospital tent. The surgeons opened my elbow, cleaned it up, shot me full of antibiotics and ordered one week of bed rest. What that really meant was one week in my pup tent that lasted about a day.

I spent that week in the command/personnel tent observing. I watched what the men there did, how they organized and got things ready for resupplying us out in the field.

On the receiving end, I had never been much impressed with the way supplies showed up: stuff all over the place, the beer and pop always hot, the ammunition just thrown together. I recorded all this in my mind—it would come in handy in a few months when disaster strikes.

CHAPTER 6

JUNGLE ROT

There are many weeks and experiences in Vietnam that I just don't remember. But I do remember the longest time we spent at one time in the field chasing the enemy around was around forty-five days. I counted everyone. I remember it was during the season when it was hot, humid and it rained a lot. The monsoon season I suppose.

I also cannot tell you if we ever had contact with the enemy, if there were any fire fights or battles or what in the world we were doing that would create such a situation that we spent that length of time away from the home base.

What I can tell you with certainty is that we were resupplied three separate times to replace our uniforms and boots. We wore them day in and day out; they literally rotted off us. The heat, the humidity and the sweat were toxic.

On that mission I got jungle rot in my crotch. To this day, fifty years later I don't wear underwear because I can't stand the feeling.

We got resupplied every three or four days with ammunition, C-rations, drinking water, pop and beer. On the resupplies that it required new uniforms and boots, they would bring in boxes of them. We piled the empty boxes, our falling-apart boots and uniforms, and burned them.

I remember one incident vividly. We were being moved from one location to another—not unusual. The helicopters came in to the LZ, on the crest of a hill or right on top. Depending on what direction the helicopters came from, you never could miss the sound of a Huey coming in. To this day when I hear one I instantly look up. When they come in they come in fast. Thump, Thump, Thump. The pilots liked to come in quickly. We loaded up and they took off fast, dropping down the side of the hill just above the tree tops until reaching a good speed, then swooping out over the valley. Their objective was getting to an altitude speedily where they weren't vulnerable to enemy fire. By staying low and going downhill to pick up speed, it was almost impossible for the enemy to hit such a moving target from any angle or any location.

We jumped on; the pilot was already taking off as we were getting situated. We were used to it.

This one time the pilot misjudged his location and air speed. The left rung of the helicopter hooked on a good-sized dead limb of a tree just as he was dropping down over the hill. We stopped in midair and just hovered there. We were hanging there, going nowhere. The pilot was trying to gain enough speed to break the limb. It wasn't happening.

I was sitting on the left back seat, next to the door with the door gunner standing in front of me. In milliseconds, I knew it would do no good for me to hang onto the door jamb, jump out on the rung and try to break the limb, because the chopper was pulling on it upward and I would be trying to break it going downward—impossible to make that happen.

I wasn't afraid to get on the rung, because that is what we did when we came into a LZ and prepared to jump off on to the ground as the helicopter came in and hovered. The only thing I could think to do was I swung my M-16 around to my left hand, put the safety off and put it on full automatic and put as many rounds as fast as I could into the limb. All the guys almost jumped out of the chopper. Instantly the limb gave way. We bucked up for a second because of all the pressure the pilot was exerting on the limb and off we went down the valley.

A few of the guys just smiled. The pilot gave me a wave over his head and never again was a word said about it. It was just one of those moments each of us rose to, without orders, to keep all of us alive.

CHAPTER 7

RIDING THE TANKS

During that first year of duty for a while we were jointly assigned to the Big Red One a famous World War II unit for an operation involving a tank battalion. It's one of the few things that I can look back on about Vietnam as fun. A lot of people don't know that tanks in some areas of Vietnam were in use a lot and were used to search and destroy the enemy.

The Viet Cong and North Vietnamese also used tanks. But they were far fewer and confined close to the border, so they could escape. Officially the U. S. couldn't go after them across the border. This was generally how things worked. But don't think for a minute that U. S. Special Forces and other covert units didn't pursue them!

We got to ride the tanks, sleep under them, walk behind them and interact with the tank crews. Most of the time the tanks were confined to the roads. But if the ground was suitable to supporting the tanks, we often took off across the fields and through the trees, looking for and chasing the enemy.

It wasn't like the enemy was just sitting around waiting for us to show up. We had overwhelming firepower, including almost constant air support from helicopter gun-

ships, jets and B-52s. When the enemy heard our tanks, they
ran away and ran quickly.

One of the most devastating things that can happen
to any group of soldiers is to get caught out in the open. The
North Vietnamese traveled mostly at night. Getting caught
in the open didn't typically happen to them. Depending on
the terrain and the circumstances, however, it was inevitable
that at some point, a large body of enemy combatants were
going to have to traverse through open country.

We knew that a battalion or regiment of NVA were
in the area somewhere. A random flight of a Huey Helicopter bringing in supplies spotted them in a cluster of trees
along an open valley. It was a coincidence. A fluke sighting.
A B-52 strike was called in. They fly so high, you don't know
they are there until you hear the explosions and feel the con-
cussion of the blast if you are close enough.

That group of enemy combatants never knew what
hit them. We heard the blasts and felt the concussions several miles away. We waited more than ten hours before we
took off to assess the damage. As we approached the area,
the smell and the smoke were over powering. From what
we could see there were no survivors. It appeared that every
single one of them had been killed. It was a horrific scene.

Normally after a battle and we cleared out, the engi-
neers came in. They bulldozed holes and pushed the enemy
dead into the holes and covered them up. That wasn't going
to happen here. It was just too big an area. There were too
many bodies.

We tried to come up with a count of the dead, but it

was impossible. There were so many body parts strung out all over a huge area, many times the size of several football fields. We estimated a number and called in over the radio and left the area to let nature take its course. I don't think there were even any souvenirs that could be salvaged: an intact AK-47, a North Vietnamese flag—there was really nothing that could be gleaned from going through the bodies, at least what was left of them.

It was the only time that I witnessed this level of carnage. The experience showed me how effectively our B-52s rained death on the Viet Cong and the North Vietnamese troops by the thousands and thousands.

THE BUS WRECK

Some things from the war you just don't forget: the sight, the smell, the reality of it and the sheer grotesquerie.

We were convoying to a different area to start another search-and-destroy mission. Three of us were sitting in the front seat of a large truck, hauling tents and other gear necessary to set up a new company staging area. We were in the lead vehicle. As we came around a corner on a highway not far from Ban Me Thuot we could see a situation up ahead.

Another large Army truck—not one from our unit— had rear-ended a bus full of Vietnamese civilians. Back then Vietnam didn't have police on the roads. To this day, in many parts of Asia, when people are loaded on a bus or a train, there is no concern for comfort or safety. As many people as possible are jammed together.

On that day fifty years ago on that jungle road, there were people on the top and hanging out the windows. The inside of the bus was packed with people standing, squeezed together or sitting on each other.

From what I could see, it only took seconds for that bus to be engulfed in flames. It was horrifying. There was nothing we could do. There was no nearby fire station, no hospital, no 911 to call. Those civilians were caught in the middle of a war. They were left to themselves. Most of them died instantly or within minutes. The bus burned for hours until we could creep around it.

There were kids, old men and old women, mothers and fathers running around screaming and crying—so horrible that you can't imagine. Eventually a couple of Vietnamese soldiers showed up and tried to restore order. But it was too late. I am sure more than a hundred individuals of all ages perished in the wreck and its hellish fire.

Eventually we were able to drive by. The putrid odor of the dead bodies mingled with the stench of the bus and the diesel nearly gagged me. The sight of all of those burned, blackened bodies has never left my memory.

PHOTOGRAPHS

A QUICK SHOWER AFTER A MISSION

WAITING TO GO OUT ON A MISSION

MY ACTUAL PACK AND BELT

RIGHT AFTER COMING OFF A MISSION

THE GENERAL PINNING ON A BRONZE STAR

CAPTURED VIET CONG AFTER A MISSION

IN MY ROOM AT AIT FT. GORDON

**NOTICE THE 4 STARS ON THE CAR
GENERAL WESTMORELAND IS WITH US**

TYPICAL REAR CAMP

FLYING THE OREGON STATE FLAG

**GETTING READY TO GO OUT IN THE FIELD
WITH THE GENERAL IN THE T-39**

HEADING OUT FOR A MISSION

PUP TENTS AT BASE CAMP

A QUIET TIME

THE FLIGHT LEAVING VIETNAM FOR GOOD

OBVIOUSLY, A HAPPY TIME

SCARED TO DEATH
ALL NIGHT LONG

I had already participated in several ambushes—why would this one be any different?

We would find a well-traveled trail that we suspected the Viet Cong, or the North Vietnamese were close by or in the area.

The NVA were North Vietnamese regulars sent from North to South. These soldiers had better weapons (usually Russian-made) and received better training (they were 'real' soldiers). NVA were official North Vietnamese Army Soldiers, The VC, or Viet Cong, were a guerrilla group funded by Soviets and the Chinese governments.

Whether they were soldiers or civilians working for the NVA or VC they traveled at night. It didn't bode well for them to travel in the day and be spotted—a magnet for a high-flying B-52 bomber or a nearby gunship.

At the same time, no ordinary civilian was going to be traveling by darkness. It made no sense. So, if you caught someone in the ambush, you were confident that he was the enemy. These night travelers might not be soldiers—they could be sympathetic civilians helping the troops, or getting paid to carry their supplies, ammunition and weapons. It made no difference. If they were in the ambush zone they were killed.

Once the location for the ambush was determined, at least four of us—no more than six—would volunteer for the ambush. The rest of the platoon or company would be off perhaps up to a mile or more from where the ambush was to take place. They would be in their perimeter for the night. Meanwhile, we would be set up on the trail, concealed and wait all night long for someone to come through the ambush area.

We would always have a minimum of two Claymore mines set up covering the trail, at least one M-60 machine gun, if not two and one M-79 grenade launcher. A few of us would have our M-16 rifles.

We never tried to determine who or what was attempting to pass—if they were coming through, they died. Simple as that. We hoped the travelers weren't more than a squad. You always ran the risk of ambushing the front of platoon or company of enemy soldiers. It was always dark, so you determined whether you opened fire or not by the amount of noise they were making. A lot of noise, you didn't open fire. This happened several times. You sensed you were completely outnumbered and out-gunned. You just had to sit and wait for them to pass. Heart thumping times. Trying not to breathe and for sure not make any noise at all. Not a situation you wanted to have to sit through more than once.

This one time six of us got set up. It got dark. We were keyed up. We took turns taking naps early on, because none of us wanted to be asleep after midnight. An ambush was not something we let new soldiers do without a good deal of experience in combat.

As darkness enveloped us we kept hearing something running through the brush. It was making grunting noises and driving us crazy. We couldn't go see what it was, open fire or even holler at it. But it was there. We had all seen and heard howler monkeys, so we knew it wasn't one or more of them.

It certainly wasn't an elephant; they just weren't in that type of terrain. It could have been a large cat. It kept running around and around, grunting and snorting and thrashing in the brush. The consensus was it wasn't a person. But it drove us mad and it scared the hell out of us. At around 2 A.M. a small group came through the ambush area. We set off both Claymore mines and opened fire with our weapons.

When the firing ceased—in less than 10 seconds—we stayed glued to our positions and did not dare move until daybreak. Then I and one of the other guys walked out from where we were concealed. The other four guys covered our flanks, front and back.

We looked around. Nothing stirred. We had killed four enemy soldiers and six supporting men carrying supplies and ammunition—and one very large wild pig. We contemplated taking the pig with us, but we had no time and you never ever stayed around an ambush that was executed after daylight.

Around this time, I was promoted to Staff Sergeant E-5 1 July, 1967.

CHAPTER 10

DISASTER STRIKES

Everyone got one week's rest and recuperation—R&R—
for the one year in Vietnam. If you extended for six months
you got another one week R&R. You also got a thirty day
leave for extending. Some destinations to choose from were
Bangkok, Tokyo, Singapore and Hawaii. Doesn't mean there
weren't more destinations to go to on an R&R. I picked Hawaii. You got to Tan Son Nhut airport by military transport,
boarded a civilian airliner and were there in hours. It was all
arranged beforehand. Normally it went smoothly. Before you
knew it, you were out of the field, on a plane, walking off that
plane and checking into a hotel on the beach in Waikiki.

I have always been a person who enjoys being out in the
sun. That was clear to me before I went into the Army. That
is why I choose Hawaii for my first R&R. It was part of me in
Vietnam and it is still a big part of my life today, even at my age.

I don't remember much about that week except my
introduction to the Cock's Roost in Waikiki, to which I
returned many, many times thereafter, during the rest of my
time in Vietnam and after returning home. It was a nice bar
upstairs, not far from off the beach and I always felt welcomed
there and always enjoyed myself.

A week later when I returned to my unit it was immediately apparent that something terrible had happened. The guys told me to come to the command tent where the Captain was waiting for me. He had something to tell me. Lt. Belding was out in the field with the rest of the platoon.

I went inside. The Captain was sitting behind his little field desk. I approached, saluted him and said: "Sergeant Scott reporting as requested, Sir." "Sit down Sergeant Scott." He said this very politely. When he looked at me I knew something was very wrong, he was almost crying.

"Sergeant Scott, a Huey is on its way in, bringing in your squad. They have all been killed. They got surrounded yesterday. It happened very quickly. They had gotten separated for a short time from the rest of the platoon." "Would you like to go with the rest of us and help get the body bags out of the chopper and into the truck." I was stunned. I couldn't say anything. I broke down and it was very tough for several minutes. The Captain got up and walked around and put his arms around me and held me for a few moments. I will never forget it. The next time I felt that sort of feeling was when my Dad held my hand during Brad's funeral, my first son who drowned at 16 months old.

It was not the first time that we had heard of this happening. Once again on the enemy's turf. In their surroundings. On their terms. A perfect set of circumstances for the enemy and they took an advantage of it. I was devastated and completely distraught.

If only I had been with them, I thought. *It wouldn't have happened.* Which was foolish. The fact of the matter was, if I had been with them then there would have been eight dead instead of seven. That would have been the end of it for me, as it was for so many others, 50,000-plus American soldiers by the end of the war.

"Sir, yes I want to help unload them." So those of us that were there walked down to the small airstrip where the choppers came in to load and unload.

Until that day it was the hardest thing I ever had to do or be a part of. When the chopper got there, it shut down its engines, so we would have no dust to deal with, or noise, which is something they rarely did. They normally landed, unloaded and were off.

It was a very solemn event for all of us as we unloaded the body bags and put them in a truck for transport to the mobile freezers and mortuary. There was nothing else that could be done by any one of us, individually or as a group. The door gunners said it was not a good situation. A couple of the guys had their heads cut off and a couple of the bodies had been mutilated.

The next few days were rough. I escaped with beer or hard liquor. I stayed drunk pretty much the whole time; everyone left me alone. On the third day the first sergeant came to me and spent some time with me. He tried to help me. He had been through World War II and the Korean War and he had seen a lot of this.

On the third day the first Sergeant asked me: "Sergeant Scott, do you want to be the one that goes to the mortuary and sign the paperwork necessary to release the bodies to be sent back to the States." "Yes" was all I said.

I will never forget that tent. The guys were laid out on cots. They had embalmed them. Cleaned them up. Sewn the heads back on. Stuffed cotton balls in the bullet holes. They all had clean uniforms on and appeared to be sleeping in body bags, with the bags unzipped down to their belt buckles.

I can still smell the embalming fluid. That whole area smelled like it all the time of course, but it was stronger with seven bodies gathered so closely. I signed all the necessary paperwork and left to go back to my area. Once again, I didn't do very well for a couple of days.

It was the second toughest thing I have ever done in my life. The first was unloading their bodies. The third toughest thing was burying Brad, my first son, who drowned in 1972.

I had fewer than sixty days or so to finish my tour. The first sergeant thought it was probably best that I not go back out into the field. He was worried that I might do something crazy. Chances are I would have. He put me on guard duty every night, so at least I was doing something. I couldn't drink on duty, so that helped. I also didn't smoke pot, as many others did while on guard duty. I slept in the morning, drank beer in the afternoon and then went on perimeter guard duty in different areas. It did help pass the time. But my emotional state wasn't getting better.

I was having a terrible time processing what had happened—and I knew it. One thing that did help me somewhat is writing to the parents of each one of the guys. For quite some time I carried on correspondence with several of their grieving parents.

Finally, the first Sergeant came to me: "Sergeant Scott, you have got to snap out of this or we are going to have recommend you get a physiological evaluation and you don't want that. This is something you are going to have to learn to deal with and accept, quickly. This needs to happen for your sake as well as all of us close to you." I knew it was time for me to get a grip on things. I thought about things for a moment and then asked. "1st Sergeant, is it possible for you to let me take over the resupply situation? I know that I can do a better job and get things streamlined and functioning properly." He immediately responded. "Yes. Do whatever it takes, I will let everyone know."

It didn't take long for me to get things squared away. It helped that every resupply was nearly identical. The ammunition included restocking M-16 ammunition, M-79 grenades, M-60 mortar rounds and Claymore mines. There were C-Rations and various other kinds of supplies. What I did differently was make sure that the various ammunitions requested was put into separate boxes; clearly marked to make it easy to get stuff passed out to the right guys.

I also got some garbage cans and took a small truck and packed the pop and beer with ice the night before the resupply was to take place. This one single thing alone improved moral in the field immensely. It was the number one thing I did that they appreciated. I also spent effort trying to make sure that any mail the guys had received went out with the resupply choppers. I made sure if there were any special requests that came in for any one guy, that it got found or accomplished and went back out on the resupply. Many times, I would even fly out on the re-supply choppers just to see the guys.

CHAPTER 11

DO I GO HOME?

It was a rough couple of months for me as my first tour of duty was approaching the end of twelve months. Since I had volunteered for the service, my commitment was three years. If you got drafted the time commitment was two years. So, if you were drafted and got sent to Vietnam after training—which, let's say, was eight months—then you would never be sent back to Vietnam. Because you didn't have enough time for another tour of duty with the few remaining months you had left. My twelve month tour added to the eight months of training meant I had plus or minus another sixteen months left.

That means if you had a critical military occupation specialty (MOS)—which I did—and you had combat experience—which I did—and that combat experience was in Vietnam—which it was—if I went home I would get a thirty day leave and get orders right back to Vietnam. We saw it happening all the time.

I got lucky. At about the end of the twelve months, when I was trying to figure out what to do, my Company Captain came to me. "Sergeant Scott, what are you going to do? Are you thinking about extending or going home and take your chances?" "Sir, I am considering extending. At least that way I know where I will come back to and what I will be doing for sure." "Sergeant, I have a suggestion. 1 Field Force is calling out for a replacement driver for Lt. General Rosson, Commander of 1 Field Force. The General wants his replacement driver to come from the 101st. I believe you would be a good one for this position. It would be worth it if you got picked for this position. The chances of you surviving another twelve month tour of duty in combat is very slim."

"Sir let's do it" is all I said.

I never knew what the requirements were. I assumed it started with someone who was levelheaded. I fit the profile in almost every area, except emotionally and I didn't wear that on my sleeve for everyone to see. Knowing the general wanted the new driver to come from the 101st meant a good number of guys were going to get interviewed. Only one would get the position. I faced tough odds.

I got close to the end of the twelve months and got paperwork allowing me to jump a helicopter to Nha Trang where I Field Force Headquarters was located. I took off with what little bit of stuff I had, which wasn't much. I turned in my weapon and my field gear. I departed wearing a pair of jungle fatigues, my jungle boots and hat, a few toilet articles and not much money.

When I got there, I checked in. They assigned me a bunk to sleep in and told me to be patient. I was told to check in every morning—the general would start seeing candidates as time allowed. I didn't see anybody else who was lingering there the way I was. The days and weeks dragged by very slowly. By the end of the third week, I was out of patience. At the end of four weeks I went in to see the sergeant and said: "Look, something is not right here. I just can't keep sitting around waiting for this. I have no clothes, no money and nothing to do."

The sergeant said, "Wait a minute—you haven't been interviewed by the general yet?"

"No," I replied. "I have been in here every morning asking when I would be interviewed, and everyone has acted as if they didn't even know I was on the list."

I was fed up, ready to go home and didn't care what happened. I needed a haircut, my uniform was shot, I had hickeys all over my neck from the whorehouses. I was broke and hung over most of the time. Nothing made any difference to me but to get the hell out of there and take my chances on coming back when and where.

I sat there for another hour. Finally, the sergeant brought a major with him, who happened to be the general's officer aide.

"Follow me," he said. He took me into to see General Rosson. He introduced me and left me standing in front of the general's desk. Now this is a three-star general. He hadn't looked up yet. I wasn't the least bit intimidated; I just wanted to go home.

When the general looked up, he got this look on his face, like what was I doing in his office. "What in the hell happened to you?" he asked me.

"Sir," I answered, "I have been waiting almost four weeks to see you. I have had only this uniform and hardly any money—only a bunk to sleep in and a place to eat. That is the way it has been since I had arrived here from out in the field. Somehow or another, those guys in the office down the hall forgot about me. But here I am."

He looked at my neck: "Well, it looks to me like you found at least one thing to do."

I never said a word. I expected to be thrown out. He sat there for a few seconds looking at me.

"Sit down," he said in a very respectful way. I saw my name on a service folder on his desk. He opened it, thumbed through some pages, looked up at me a few times and then closed it. A few more seconds went by.

"Let's talk," he said, as if I were the most important person in the world. I almost started crying. Because I was still so emotional from the experience with the death of my squad and having waited so long to speak with the general, I had a tough time maintaining my composure. But I did.

It didn't take long for us to create a bond between us. A bond that was to last throughout my relationship with him, which was a good year. We were both from Oregon— he from Portland, I from Bend. He had graduated from the University of Oregon; I thought I was going to. When I told him the circumstances of my departure from the University of Oregon, he got a good laugh out of the story. His father was still alive and living in Portland; my father was living in Bend. He was in his early forties. As a young Lieutenant he had been decorated for combat valor at the Anzio Beachhead in Italy during World War II. He was a soldier's soldier. I had just turned twenty.

We had a great conversation and it set the stage for a very good relationship between a three-star General and an E-5 soldier. He never once brought up the situation with my squad and never once did he make it a topic of the conversation. I do remember him saying I had a rough time of it and he respected that.

Fifteen minutes later he called in the major. I can't remember the major's name. I should, as you will see later, but for the life of me I can't.

General Rosson told the major very briskly, that I was going to be his new driver. The major was to see that I got my orders and some pay for the thirty days leave home. Further, he was to personally fly me down to Saigon, Tan Son Nhut airfield in his jet, a T-39, so I could take my thirty day leave. The major was not only the general's officer's aide but also his pilot.

That fifteen minute conversation changed my life in so many positive ways. It probably saved my life from having to return for another year of combat with the 101st. However, as this story unfolds, the general came closer to getting me killed on one of his trips I accompanied him on than anything I had encountered in the field.

CHAPTER 12

THE GENERAL'S NEW DRIVER

After spending almost thirteen plus months in Vietnam, I remember only several things that took place during my month-long leave home. It is not an unusual thing for me to have no memory of periods of time in my life as I have mentioned. There are many such gaps in my life after which I do not remember a single thing. I have no idea what the cause is. I have given up trying to figure it out. Was I too detached at the time, too many brain cells destroyed by all the alcohol for a length of time up until I turned fifty, or did I just tune it all out? Did my mother drop me on my head and didn't tell anyone?

I have given up on trying to figure out why or trying to remember what took place during these lapses of memory. After all, what difference does it make in the overall scheme of things.

There is one Oregon memory on that thirty day leave. During my first year in Vietnam, I had written the State of Oregon and asked for an Oregon state flag to fly over my hooch/tent or wherever I happened to be. Once I found out that Oregon had no such program and did not provide flags to active members of the military. I decided to change that.

In the meantime, I had my Mother get me one and send it over in one of the Sweet Tooth packages. Sweet Tooth was a program that my Mother and other mothers of soldiers from the Bend, Oregon area started. They would bake cookies and make candy. They would buy toilet articles, books, girlie magazines and send them to us at various time of the year. Bennie Dexter's mother was one of the first mothers to help get this started and was actively involved for many years as the war lingered on.

I had made an appointment with Governor McCall in Salem, Oregon the first week I had gotten home for the leave. With the war going on and what all, he had no choice but to meet with me. I asked him to initiate a program to provide Oregon state flags to every member of the Armed Services who requested one, free of charge. That program is still in existence today and is administered by the Secretary of State.

Once back in Vietnam, I was now in training as the personal driver for Lieutenant General William B. Rosson, Commander of I Field Force. There was Ambassador Bunker, General Westmoreland, then his Chief of Staff General Abrams and then General Rosson. I spent my first two weeks with his temporary driver, because the driver I was replacing had already rotated back to the States.

There really wasn't much to get oriented to and learn:

- keep the car full of gas, clean and waxed up;

- always wear starched jungle fatigues with polished boots;

- never get caught not wearing your head gear while driving;

- always communicate with the general's staff so you knew what the general's schedule was;

- never be late to pick him up—never;

- always know where you are going and how to get back.

Each morning the general would bound out of his house full of energy. I would have the door open for him. He would get in. I would shut the door, go around the back of the car, get in and away we would go. His headquarters had a long stairway up to where his office was, so I would pull in front of that stairway. By the time I got out and around the back of the car to open his door he usually was already headed up the stairs. I would shut the door and go park in my parking spot and start waxing and polishing the car. Once I got that routine down, sometimes I would go up and sit in the staff's office and figure out what was going on. There I got to meet everyone who was anybody. The general always kept his door shut. He was a very busy and he commanded a lot of troops and had a lot of responsibility. You must visualize the circumstances. Being the three-star General's driver, the General in the position of third in command of an entire war in Vietnam put you, his driver in one hell of a position to see, hear and do just about anything you wanted to.

Many times, General Westmoreland or General Abrams flew in to see General Rosson. From 1964 to 1968 William C. Westmoreland commanded all U. S. Army forces in Vietnam.

Every time one of them would fly in, General Rosson would go with me out to the airport to meet the plane, pick them up and drive them back to headquarters for their briefings. Or sometimes we went to 5th Special Forces headquarters or the ARVN's headquarters (South Vietnamese) or the Korean's headquarters. Sometimes we went to the house for lunch. Sometimes General Abrams stayed overnight, but I do not remember General Westmoreland ever staying overnight. I remember General Abrams very well, because he had me make his gin and tonics in the mornings and in the evenings.

In one of the photos, if you will notice the four stars on the left side of the bumper, this meant General Westmoreland was in the car. Lt. General Rosson in the car required three stars on the plate.

One time we went out to the airport to pick up General Westmoreland. I thought I would take a short cut on the way back out of the airport by going through the Vietnamese, ARVN's part of the airport. I got lost. I didn't have a clue how to get back on track and get these two generals back to General Rosson's headquarters. It was a nightmare. I finally had to stop and ask some guys how to get out of there—you talk about being embarrassed. Fortunately, they had a lot to talk about and nothing was said to me. I do remember General Rosson with a smile on his face when he exited the car.

Every so often Ambassador Ellsworth Bunker also flew in for briefings and meetings, though not nearly as often as General Westmoreland or General Abrams. There were not too many times when something wasn't going on every day.

The complex we lived in had several very nice houses, a small PX, an officer's club and an enlisted man's club. It was approximately three miles from the Headquarters building. It was close to a large block in size. I stayed in a room that was kind of off to the side in the back of another house right next door. My shower was an outdoor shower. I had a bathroom, hot and cold water, and the living conditions were above average.

I also got to eat the same food as the general. I went into the kitchen where his two cooks did the cooking, I sat at a table and ate like a king. In this house, the cooks had rooms and his enlisted aide also had a room. The general's officer's aide stayed in the house with him.

His chief of staff was a two-star general—I don't remember his name but can recall his face. He had his own house and driver. In one of the chapters I will tell a story about the chief of staff's driver during the TET Attack.

The general sometimes flew out after his morning briefings and was gone all day long. He and the major would take the T-39 or they would take his helicopter. The major did not fly the helicopter. The general had his own helicopter pilots and if I remember correctly they were always the same pilots. The general was very active and liked to go out in the field and meet with his commanders to get first-hand reports during firefights and battles.

When there was down time and the major knew he had time, we would go out to the airport and take the general's plane, the T-39, down to Saigon and pick up lobster, steaks, Heineken beer, Chivas Regal Scotch and anything else the cooks needed that was unusual. As I said, I ate like a king and drank like a king. Working for a three-star general presented me with extravagant perks that I could only have dreamed about in the field. I must say, I never missed an opportunity to enjoy.

One of the impressive things about General Rosson was he was personable. He was not aloof, was not gruff and was always respectful.

He rose at 4:30 A.M. and ran for thirty minutes every single morning. It wasn't long before I was running with him. He encouraged me to run alongside—never in the back or off to the right as other generals expected of their subordinates. We would run from one end of the complex to the other, back and forth and back and forth. No one was ever out there running with us, which always amazed both of us because it was the best part of our day. The run gave us time to talk, plan the day's events and just have a conversation. One of the most pleasant things I remember about that experience was him saying every morning as we parted after the run, "See you in a while."

Only one time was the general upset with me: when I got the "clap" from a whorehouse—gonorrhea. He noticed that I was having trouble sitting behind the steering wheel of the car and asked me, no, *he demanded* to know, "What the hell is wrong with you?"

I had to tell him. "I had to go to sick call," I said. I told him I got a shot of penicillin in the butt and it was very sore.

When we got to the house, he ordered me to go upstairs with him to his bedroom. He walked over, pulled open a drawer in his dresser and threw me a pack of prophylactics. "You'd better not let that happen again," was all he said, in a firm voice. That was it. He never said another word. Until my butt was better I didn't move around in the driver's seat any more than I had to.

When I knew General Rossen was going to be gone all day, once I got him to the airport, I was free. I had no other responsibilities. So long as the car was full of gas, clean and shined and I knew what time to be back to the airport to pick him up, the day was all mine. I had nobody else to report to or answer to. Once I did what personal chores I had to do, I was off to the beach.

One attractive feature about Nha Trang was that it was a world-class beach resort. It is to this day. Our complex was less than a block and a half off the beach. All I had to do was park the car under the car port in front of his house and head to the beach. This little expedition included a cooler filled with half a case of beer. Another convenience was a fine little corner bar, just across from the beach just down the block from the security gate to our complex. They played Frank Sinatra music all the time. I will never forget it.

I had to be careful. If I sat at the beach and drank beer all day, chances are by the time the general arrived back at the airport I was half drunk and sometimes loaded.

Only one time did he say anything and that was when I forgot to put my hat on when I got out of the car to make sure the door was open for him when he came out of the jet. I was more than pretty loaded that afternoon. He hurried down the stairs, I had the door open for him and he got right into the back seat. He always sat on the passenger side in the back. I shut the door, trotted around to the driver's door and off we went.

This time he never took his eyes off me as he came down the stairs of the jet. For the life of me I couldn't figure out what was going on. What was he thinking? I knew when we got in the car.

"Sergeant Scott. Don't ever forget to have your head gear on when you pick me up," he said. He reminded me it was a sign of respect. "You do respect me, don't you?"

"Yes, sir," I replied as I grabbed my hat laying on the seat next to me. That was it—again, not another word at any time. After that I never forgot to wear my hat.

CHAPTER 13

HAPPY NEW YEAR...
THE TET OFFENSIVE

On the afternoon of January 30, 1968 at about 6:30 in the early evening, I was taking a shower. The south wall to my outdoor shower was also a retaining wall which separated the compound to a house in which a Vietnamese family lived on the corner. The compound was a rectangular block of buildings—but in the southeast corner this house was not part of the compound. It had a cement-block wall adorned with barbed wire around the top.

Do I ever remember seeing this Vietnamese family who lived there? Probably. How could one not? Do I ever remember them doing anything out of the ordinary? No. I lived right next to them for months.

I was almost done with the shower and I heard what sounded like firecrackers going off.

Sounds like someone is celebrating Tet early, I thought. Tet is the annual Vietnamese lunar New Year. This year we were expecting nothing other than the normal party. We had been briefed on what to expect, which was nothing. It was normal for the setting off a ton of firecrackers. I grabbed a chair and stood on it, looking over the wall.

"Knock it off," I hollered and stepped down. The *bang-bang-bang* continued.

I paused. *That sure sounds like an AK-47,* I thought. I had heard that sound often enough. I got dried off, put on some fatigues and a pair of flip flops, and walked out of the driveway of the house.

I was startled to see the military police guarding the front gate to the compound returning fire from behind barricades. They were struggling to get the gate closed—they were taking serious fire. I rushed back to my room, grabbed my boots, helmet, flak jacket and AR-15 and all the ammo I had and rushed back out to help the MPs. By the time I got back out there they had the gate closed.

If there weren't too many attackers, we agreed, we could hold them off until reinforcements showed up. We were very perplexed and bewildered on what was going on. For hours, we took fire. No one got hit—which was just luck.

After dark, the firing continued. We figured out that most of the enemy firing was coming out of the house on the corner. The house that my shower was on the other side of their wall. The wall I had stood on the chair and told them to "knock it off." The driveway to that house was on the east side of the "rectangle." You couldn't see it from the entrance gate to the compound. They were going back and forth out of the driveway of the house and crossing over to the other side of the street that ran along the south side of the compound, where the entrance gate was and firing at us from there.

The two-star general—General Rosson's chief of staff—and his driver both lived in our compound. The driver for the Chief of Staff found a ladder and got up on top of the garage on the border of the south side of the compound. It was dark by now. It was on the east side of the compound as well, which put it right next to the back yard where the enemy troops were holed up.

I am sure his thinking was that if he got on the roof, up there in the dark, he could see right down on them— either in the house or in the back yard. That was true. But once he fired that of course gave away his position. He was immediately hit in the head. He didn't have his helmet on.

What a mess. If you got back far enough, you could see him lying on the top of the roof of the garage, which wasn't that high. He was bleeding badly. Only a matter of time and he was going to bleed out.

There was security lighting on the compound's perimeter. The attack was going on all over the town, so there was also flares going off all over the place from artillery, mortars or whatever. There was plenty of light from both the security lighting and flares in the sky.

Everyone else was busy. I thought the only thing to do was go get him off the roof. I got someone to hold the ladder, went up and crawled on my belly to where he was lying. I grabbed the back of his collar and dragged him back to the ladder, climbed on the ladder, put him over my shoulder and got him down that way. He was fairly thin, so he wasn't that heavy. Once we got him on the ground, we had a medic do for him what he could.

I don't know how he got to the hospital. I don't know if he got there quickly or what the circumstances were. I do know that we were under constant attack for that night and had to deal with the attack for a good two days. During those two-plus days, we had to stay in the compound. It was just too dangerous to take the general to his office. He was not happy about that.

I went up to the second story of the general's house, made my way into the attic and through a hole in the roof. I hid behind the pitch of the roof, firing down into the house in the corner and throwing grenades. I did this for two days in a row several times a day.

On the third day it was safe enough to go to the office. I remember it vividly because it was the only time I drove the car wearing a helmet and flak jacket with a loaded AR-15 sitting next to me. I remember hearing sniper fire and hearing shooting still going on while our soldiers and the ARVN's were taking care of what remained of the enemy in the city.

Keep in mind that this three-star general for whom I drove wasn't afraid of anything. If he was afraid he wasn't ever going to show it. He wanted to go home, back to his house for lunch on that third day.

Okay I thought, but I wasn't excited about driving when I knew there were still enemy snipers in the area. We drove back to the compound. When I got him back, one of the MPs motioned to me to talk to him and said, "You've got to come around here and look at this."

It was the house that sat on the outside corner of our compound that he wanted to show me.

We walked out of the gate, turned left and rounded the corner and walked through the driveway opening into the house. What was in there was unbelievable. There were more than forty dead Viet Cong and North Vietnamese soldiers. I have never forgotten the sight. They were stacked up under the beds, in the closets, all over the place. They had been trapped. The amount of fire they took and the number of grenades that were thrown in there—including some by me—didn't give them a chance.

I was astounded. I felt lucky that these guys hadn't been more organized and hadn't figured out a way to get into the compound at night and hit us then.

Now we knew that the enemy had been bringing men and weapons into this house for a long time. They were storing the weapons and preparing to participate in the Tet Offensive. For months. Right next door.

I went back into the general's house, interrupted his lunch and told him he must take the time before we left to let me take him around and show him what was in the house next door. I remember like it was yesterday he and I walking out of his house, out the gate, down the street, around the corner and into the house. Once in the house, he was absolutely astounded.

"It's a good thing these guys didn't wait and get into the compound over the back fence, through your shower and hit us that way," he said.

Once back in his office, General Rosson called the South Korean General, with whom he met with often and asked him to send some soldiers around to clean up the house. The South Korean soldiers are tough and ruthless. They showed up with a dump truck, pitch forks and cleaned the house out. They took the bodies to a soccer field where they had bulldozed a huge hole.

The Tet Offensive was a coordinated attack on most major cities in South Vietnam by the Viet Cong and the North Vietnamese—including Saigon. It was a devastating military loss for them. They lost upwards of 17,000 soldiers; whereas the Americans lost 4,954 between Jan 30th and March 28th which was the end of the first phase of the Tet Offensive. The body counts didn't matter. What mattered is that Tet showed the ordinary South Vietnamese citizens that the whole country was vulnerable—no place was safe. The American public gave up on the war and Nixon prepared to end it.

One month after I thought I heard firecrackers in the shower, half a world away, influential CBS anchorman Walter Cronkite told his American audience that "we are mired in a stalemate" in Vietnam. It could only, he said, "be ended by negotiation, not victory."

I had started to get bored several weeks before Tet and had asked the general if I could go along on his daily routine: flying out into the field to meet with his commanders and troops.

About the fifth or sixth day after the beginning of the Tet Offensive, General Rosson decided to fly to Bam Me Thuot, which was always in the thick of battle in that area.

There was an ARVN, South Vietnamese Command post there. He asked me if I would like to go. What we didn't know at the time we took off was they were under imminent attack by a regiment of North Vietnamese.

We flew there in the T-39. Probably didn't take thirty minutes. There was the general, the major and me. We landed on the airfield; no other planes or helicopters were on the runway or parked anywhere. All three of us noticed that, but we didn't pay much attention. We were picked up by three Jeeps which were ARVN driven, one of us in each vehicle and headed to the headquarters for a briefing that the general had requested.

As always, there were Special Forces officers and men around. One of the Special Forces guys pulled me aside said: "You guys don't want to stay here very long. We are expecting an attack. In fact, we are expecting to be overrun."

I immediately went inside, pulled the Major aside and told him what I had been told. He was very upset and showed it. But we were in a very delicate position. Neither one of us wanted to barge into the briefing, grab the general and carry him out of there. We decided that the major would go back to the plane and get it started, the door open and pointed down the runway, ready to take off.

I would wait until the last moment possible, go in and tell the general we had to leave. We would head back to the airport in the other two Jeeps. Both jeeps had both drivers sitting in them, running at the bottom of the steps to the building in which they were holding the briefing. When I heard the first AK-47 rounds coming through the trees, I went in and walked right into the meeting room.

"Sir," I saluted and said, "we need to leave, and we need to leave right now."

He knew me well enough to not question my sense of urgency. He didn't say a word. He stood. We walked out and down the steps. He got in the first Jeep on the passenger side. I got in the second Jeep but sat in the back, so I could look both our both sides and backward. As we were driving to the airport, we could see the North Vietnamese troops moving through the trees toward the headquarters. AK-47 rounds were going everywhere.

The major was ready for us. I didn't even get time to shut the door before he was already barreling down the runway. I sat behind the general. Nobody said anything until we were in the air. Then I said to the General, "Sir, with all due respect, I don't think I am going to go with you anymore."

He nodded his head. "That was close, wasn't it?" he said.

The next time he headed out to visit the troops I went back to my routine of going to the beach.

A couple of weeks later the general suggested that we go to the hospital to see the Chief of Staff's driver, who had gotten shot in the head. He was the one I had carried off the roof. We walked into his hospital room and instantly had a sense that he recognized us, even though he was in a complete vegetative state of mind. He couldn't talk. He just grunted and kept grabbing at his crotch. It was a very hard time for both the General and myself. As we walked away, we both had tears in our eyes. We got in the car and I turned the key.

"Sergeant Scott," said the general, "if you are ever with me and that happens to me, you make sure I don't make it to the hospital. Please."

"Sir," I replied, "please do the same for me."

We drove back to the compound in complete silence, each of us completely over come with grief.

CHAPTER 14

MOVING DAY

Probably the biggest event to come out of the Tet Offensive affecting both General Rosson's life and indirectly mine was the fact that General Westmoreland relieved Lieutenant General Cushman of his command. General Robert E. Cushman, Jr. had commanded the U. S. Marines; now General Rosson was in command of the Marines. I believe this was one of the few times in the history of the Marines or the Army that a commanding general from the Army was in command of Marines. There was a time in World War II when a Marine commander was in command of some of the Army in the South Pacific.

The marines continued taking heavy losses up around Da Nang and Hué. We were to pack up and go to Phu Bai. General Rosson became Commanding General, Provisional Corps (later XXIV Corps), Vietnam, 10 March 1968 – 31 July 1968 a three-division force concentrated in the northern two provinces of South Vietnam. This is in the northern part of I Corps not far from the DMZ.

We settled into Phu Bai in a compound that wasn't nearly as comfortable or big as the one in Nha Trang. In fact, we were immediately subject to weekly mortar and rocket fire from the North Vietnamese. We could retreat to sand-bag bunkers behind the house. The general's headquarters and office were also surrounded by bunkers.

I slept in a small room, no bigger than a closet in the back of the house. I had to go down to the MP's barracks to take a shower. I did have access to a toilet in the house. Initially and throughout the time we were in Phu Bai I didn't have much driving to do. The circumstances and conditions were different. In fact, I don't know if we even took the car—I think we just took a jeep.

By the time we got set up in Phu Bai I had about a month left on my first sixth month extension.

What a broad experience my extension was as the General's driver, despite the experience of the Tet Offensive and my trip to Ban Me Thuot with the General. The likely alternative—going back out in the field—also played into my gratitude for the General giving me the experience as his driver. I don't remember any bad times. Things were calm, routine and I never really knew what he was doing or what was going on, except what little bit I picked up in his office, and what his staff was doing. I had a security clearance. It wasn't a top-priority one though, so I don't remember any conversations in the car between him and General Westmoreland or other Generals who flew in to meet him. I regret that I didn't become more engaged and find out more what was going on and why. But I didn't. I just did my job, stayed out of the radar and flew low.

I knew that my six months was going by fast and I was going to be faced with the same decision I did six months ago: do I extend another time or go home and take my chances?

I was twenty-seven months into my three-year commitment. With eight months of training, thirteen months during my first tour of duty and now the six month extension, which got me to twenty-seven months. That left another nine months—not quite enough to worry about getting sent back for a full year's tour of duty, but it sure as hell was enough time to send me back for a six month tour of duty. This was happening quite often.

Since I had a critical military occupation specialist designation, eighteen months of Vietnam experience and was eligible to be promoted to E-6. Getting promoted meant I could easily get sent to a platoon and be a platoon sergeant. In fact, I haven't mentioned it yet, but the general wanted to promote me to E-6 and I told him that I felt there were guys out in the field that deserved the E-6 stripes a great deal more than I did.

If I did go home and by some chance got sent back it would be with the 101st I was sure. But I knew of guys that were sent to the 82nd Airborne after being with the 101st. Worse yet you could be assigned to the 173rd Airborne which did most of the dirty work for General Westmoreland.

Of course, I knew somebody I could talk to about this. He could help just about make anything happen. That conversation took place at 5:15 A.M. on one of our runs after moving to Phu Bai.

Along with trying to decide if I was going to extend for the second time, I also was eligible for another R&R.

During the conversation with General Rosson about me extending for the 2nd time, he told me I was eligible for another R&R and deserved it and should take it.

He said, "Just make sure I have a temporary driver I can rely on when you take your R&R and your 30 day leave you will take when you extend.

A week later I was in Hawaii sipping a beer at the Cock's Roost.

CHAPTER 15

A LOCAL GIRL

When it came time for me to extend my tour in Vietnam the 2nd time I decided to go to Australia for my thirty days leave rather than go home. The "temporary" driver we used for my R&R week was still available, so he took over and I headed out to Australia for thirty days.

I spent the entire month in Perth, on the beach and rented a small apartment right on the beach. Of course, a month gives one some time to integrate with the locals. I had no problem doing that. Meeting a "local girl" was also not a problem, especially with my being from America and on leave from fighting in Vietnam—the opportunities for female companionship were limitless. I settled on a girl named Gwen Harrold, about my age, blond, blue-eyed and of course she filled the bill in all the ways one was looking for. I even spent some time at her house, with her parents.

When it was time to leave, leaving was difficult. But leave I did. The plane stopped in Singapore. For some reason I got off the plane. I don't remember if it was a scheduled stopover or mechanical problems. Doesn't make any difference what the reason was. All that matters is I got off the plane and didn't get back on that one or any other one.

I went downtown and hawked my movie camera and a few other things and got tied up with a one Miss Sophia Abdulla. 3 weeks went by all too quickly. Those three weeks meant I was absent without leave—AWOL— late for returning to Vietnam and for sure returning to duty as General Rosson's driver. I was in trouble. I knew it. There was nothing I could do but catch a plane and go face the music.

When I got to Vietnam I called the general's office and he told them to tell me I could get back on my own. I had to go out to the airport. It took me two days to catch a ride back to Phu Bai on a C-130 flight.

Once back to the office, the general wouldn't talk to me or see me, but he did manage to get me assigned to "personnel." So here I was again, behind a typewriter, shuffling paper work and wondering what my fate was. He did let me know in a roundabout way that he had replaced me as his driver, taking the temporary driver as his permanent driver.

I am about ready to relate an experience that I believe I have told only one other time and that was when I was going through therapy at the Veterans Clinic in Las Vegas for my final evaluation as one hundred percent Post Traumatic Stress Disorder. I think this experience is what prompted the doctor to designate me "permanent and decisive."

A major who was running the personnel division office where I was assigned took a liking to me. He was probably in his late thirties, maybe early forties. I remember him being kind of a big-gutted guy. Nice guy but by no means a tested combat officer. We went to lunch together. We went drinking together at the officer's club. We spent a fair amount of time together. Most people in the officer's club thought I was still the general's driver so I could go in and out as I pleased. That privilege came back to haunt me.

After one night of hard drinking with the major, I opened my eyes in his room—he was molesting me!

I was shocked. I was angry. I ran outside and passed out behind the barracks. I slept it off and made my way back to my room. I took a shower and went to work. I could see the major was already in his office. I didn't recognize his presence. Not a word. Not a glance. All I will say is two days later the major did not show up for duty.

This experience affected me deeply. Throwing it in with the shock of my squad all being killed months before, I clearly had some psychological issues to deal with.

Several weeks after the nighttime barracks episode, General Rosson called me in: "Was I was ready to go back to work? "That is all he said.

At that moment, I thought he meant back to being his driver. He informed me that he was making me his en-listed aide. Talk about being shocked and excited at the same time. I was to learn the ropes during the coming week from his current aide, whom I knew well.

Not a word was ever spoken about my having been AWOL.

CHAPTER 16

BANISHED TO THE AMMO DUMP

As the weeks and months went by, I didn't hear anything about Lieutenant General Rosson's imminent rotation back to the Pentagon. I am sure some of his staff knew, but he called us all in one morning and told us his time was up. He was being replaced by Lt. General Stilwell.

Lt. General Richard G. Stilwell had quite a personal history. He was heavily involved in the war, especially the Fifth Special Forces.

This man was, in certain circles, not very well liked or respected. He was crude, rude and belligerent—he looked it, he walked it and he acted it.

I had two months remaining on my time in country—then I would be on my way home for good.

The little room I had in the back of the house was my little sanctuary. I never spent much time with General Stilwell, never did I go on any trips with him, nor did he involve me in anything. I knew he was in the process of finding my replacement. That individual was picked, and I made sure the new aide understood the policies and procedures expected of him.

This was difficult to articulate to my replacement because my benchmark was what General Rosson had expected. I didn't really have a clue what General Stilwell's expectations were—nor did I care.

About a month before my tour was up, I disappeared into the whiskey. Lord knows why, because I wasn't a whiskey drinker but a beer drinker. I started drinking early in the day almost every day. What I relate here is only what my replacement told me the morning after and what transpired from my Summary Court Martial.

I had access to the officer's club. I walked through the door early one evening and berated a pair of two-star generals, who happened to have a couple of Vietnamese ladies with them. I don't know if they were ladies of the night or not, but that was a moot point. I called them all kind of names and told both generals to get fucked.

When I finally woke up in my room the next morning, I was a muddy and muddled mess. My replacement was sitting in a chair waiting for me to wake up.

Here is close to the way the conversation went. "Sergeant Scott, you are in big trouble. Do you realize what you did?" "No," I said, "I don't remember anything." "You told a couple of two-star Generals to get fucked and insulted the women they were with." "Then you almost got into a fight with another officer when he tried to get you outside." "You are really in trouble." "They had to call the MP's, and have you arrested." "It is a good thing you know the MP's, or they might have had to hurt you in order to get you to settle down and go with them."

I never got too excited about anything. I was way too hung over to get excited about this. He went on. "The MP's aren't happy that you woke up and walked out of their jail." The MP's hadn't locked the door because they knew me and figured I wouldn't wake up anyway.

The last thing he said was: "The General is going to be calling you into his office, so you had better get ready to go see him. He is very pissed off."

Mid-morning General Stilwell called me into his office. He made me stand at attention. "Sergeant Scott, I don't know what got into you, but it is not something I am going to tolerate. I worry about someone that drinks as much as you do alone. I have no other choice but to set an example and court martial you. Until then, you are not to leave the compound and you are not to drink. Dismissed." He must have been paying more attention to what I was doing than I thought.

The General Court Martial took less than a week to arrange.

When I walked into the office for the court martial hearing, guess who was the presiding judge for the court martial? General Rosson's officer aide whom I knew very well. We were both shocked at seeing each other. He fined me twenty-five dollars. That was it—took about five minutes. Of course, he had a lot of personal information about me to draw on. The major and I had spent a good deal of time together when he was General Rosson's officer's aide and pilot. We were friends, at least as good as anyone could have been in Vietnam; considering he was an officer and I was an enlisted man.

Two hours later General Stilwell called me into his office. He was livid. He was so upset I thought he was going to have a heart attack. Once again, he made me stand at attention in front of his desk. There was nobody else in the room.

"Sergeant Scott, I don't know what happened or how this came about, but I am pulling Command Influence here. You are hereby a private. I am taking all your medals away from you. Since there isn't enough time for you left in Vietnam to go back out in the field, you are to go on guard duty out at the ammo dump until you leave. Dismissed."

I didn't mind. Shortly thereafter, several days I think it was, the guys in personnel got hold of me and told me to not worry about the court martial papers or the demotion or taking away my medals—all the paperwork had disappeared. Nothing had been put into the system or into my file or sent anywhere. Having friends in the right place paid off. I had always treated everybody with respect, helped where I could—here and now was my reward.

CHAPTER 17

TIME TO GO HOME

By now, Oct 1968 there weren't too many American enlisted men who had spent as much time in Vietnam as I had. They were out there, but not many.

I never shed a tear. Goodbyes were said, hands shaken, the last beer drained. I got a ride to Da Nang and boarded a plane to Saigon, Tan Son Nhut airport and was issued orders for my Pan Am flight home.

When you went on an R&R, a thirty day leave or on your final flight home, you always were required to wear khakis, the tan-colored uniform. Your jump boots were to be highly shined. You were airborne and expected to look sharp.

No weapon, no packs, no nothing but your paperwork and a few personal items. You got in line, headed out on the tarmac, climbed the stairs into the plane and found a seat. It was just like you did on the R&R's and thirty day leaves. Just like you were going on vacation.

Except this time, you knew you weren't coming back.

You could take a duffel bag and if I remember correctly that duffel bag was never searched. That is how the guys took souvenirs home. I took an old rifle I had got off a VC to give to my Dad.

There were basically two kinds of soldiers who got to experience the feeling of climbing those steps for the last time: Those of us who saw combat and those who didn't. There were those of us who knew and those that didn't have a clue.

When I sat down in one of the middle seats and looked to my left, I almost died. There was Hal Stromholt—Sergeant Stromholt of the United States Army. I went to the University of Oregon with Hal. I had not heard from him or seen him since. He was from New Hampshire. If I remember correctly his great-grandfather had been an ambassador to France. He wanted to be a journalist. That's what he was doing in the Army, reporting for the Stars and Stripes. We were both shocked and over joyed with seeing each other. He had been drafted and this was his flight home. We just couldn't believe it.

I have not before now said anything about this part my life, but throughout my time in Vietnam I was engaged to marry a girl from Roseburg, Oregon. I knew her at the University of Oregon. Her name was Carol Jeppensen. She had been waiting patiently for me to return.

By the time we landed in Tokyo to refuel, the pilot was standing in front of Hal and me in the aisle. "Guys, you have got to settle down. The stewardesses are scared. They think you are crazy and are not sure what you are going to do. They are not going to serve you any more alcohol. If you don't give me your word, I will have to put you off the plane. That means you miss your date to get out of the Army and that is not something you want to do." Both Hal and I agreed to settle down. We ended up sleeping the rest of the way to Ft. Lewis, Washington.

My mother and Mrs. Ede McKlennan, a longtime family friend, were going to pick me up at Fort Lewis. Washington. Hal had plans to catch a flight from Seattle to an airport close to his home in New Hampshire.

By the time we landed at Fort Lewis, we had decided that we were going to go to Europe. I would spend three days in Bend, go to Roseburg and break off the engagement. He would go to New Hampshire, spend three days saying hello to his family and packing. We would meet in New York on our way to London.

Exactly seven days from departing Vietnam, Hal and I were in London. We purchased a Volkswagen Bug and were driving around England, looking over maps, deciding where we were going and what we were going to see. We spent eight months traveling around Europe.

MY BROTHER'S
SPECIAL FORCES TEAM

VIET NAM-U.S. ARMY GREEN BERET
NOV. 1970-NOV. 1971
SGT. STEVEN C. SCOTT
MAC V SOG
STUDIES AND OBSERVATION GROUP

My intention is to not get vivid or explicit about my brothers Steve's experiences in Vietnam. But to share the highlights, help share some of his story on his experiences during his 1-year tour of duty with the U.S. Army Green Berets.

Steve had just returned from a snowy but successful elk hunt with our Dad in the Minim River County in NE Oregon. The winter weather caused a several days delay in his return to Oregon State University. That delay caused Steve to miss all his mid-term exams.

He was frustrated with school and goofed off too much and was always scrambling to get passing grades. Like me, he decided it was time to move on since he never did have any patience. He volunteered at an Army recruiting station in Corvallis, Oregon and was in boot camp by late November 1968. He excelled in boot camp as he was in pretty good shape and lean. He was older than most at twenty and had a strong back ground on the farm and all the hunting and fishing gave him a competitive edge. At this time I was traveling in Europe.

Because of his success in boot camp he ended up taking the test to see if he was suited to be in the elite Special Forces group. They recruited him for the program and he was off to Fort Gordon, Georgia for Advanced Infantry training and then jump school at Fort Benning. Then to Fort Bragg, North Carolina for Special Forces boot camp for ten weeks. The program was not for those whom did not want to be there and about half usually washed out. He was trained in all weapons and cross trained as a medic and intelligence for another six months.

He also jumped in Alaska in the middle of winter on Gulcana Glazier out of Fairbanks and he showed me a card he received, and it was fifty-two degrees below zero. It was a cold weather training which none of them understood why, because all of them were off to Viet Nam in ninety degree temperature a few weeks later.

He arrived in county through Long Bin and proceeded to Da Nang where the Fifth Special Forces Group Headquarters was located. I have mentioned when I worked for the General as his driver and personal enlisted aide, we would go to this Headquarters quite often. Since I had left Vietnam in October 1968 there was no chance of us running into each other.

No one knew where or what was in front of them until they were processed and assigned. Steve was assigned to Thong Duc AQ-109 which was a compound of about two-hundred and fifty indigenous personnel trained and managed by the twelve or so American Special Forces.

Their mission was to control the surrounding area out to about twenty-five miles in all directions. A-109 was at the northern most A-site in the country and was only about forty miles from the DMZ and ten miles from the Laos border. This was the main route for the NVA (North Vietnamese Army) to move their troops and supplies to the south.

This was the time of the war that the turmoil was at its height at home with anti- war sentiment. In hind-sight the North Vietnamese were staging for their major push to get the American troops out of the South. There were very few regular ARMY or MARINES Units out in the jungle or field in the northern sectors, so the North Vietnamese could do what they wanted to do without a lot of harassment from the Americans.

About two months prior to his arrival at Thong Duc the NVA began a siege of the A-Site by pounding the site with mortar and 120 MM rounds in the amount of about ten per day and this continued for most of the time he was there. This random incoming of mortar rounds was their greatest risk of being injured as they did not know when they were coming except that the outside perimeter guards would fire their rifles as a warning of incoming when they heard the initial pop of the mortar round off in the distance.

They had secure fortified concrete bunkers that the Sea Bees had built in the mid-sixties. They all would scramble into the bunkers when they had incoming. He only went outside this camp two times during his time at Thong Duc. The excursions outside were to discover or attempt to sweep the area in and around the camp.

When they did go out three Americans would take about thirty to forty indigenous men with them to engage the enemy. They would stay out in front of the Americans until contact and then duck and call in air strikes for them. He only experienced sniper fire one time outside the perimeter of the A site. The scary part of a sniper is the unknown of when and where it will come from. You do not know it has happened unless you're hit. It never seemed fair that we had that advantage of air support and the NVA did not. Part of his frustration was our superiority of equipment and intelligence but our lack of will politically to use it like it could have been used. If we would have really used our assets he outcome would have been success and freedom for the South Vietnamese.

None of his team were killed (several were wounded) during the two months he was there. About six months after he left Thong Duc when the Americans turned over the responsibility to the South Vietnamese and they left the site. This was one of the first locations to totally fall into the hands of the North right before the fall of Saigon and the Country.

Steve then volunteered and went to CCN (Command and Control North) in Da Nang to run recon. He was assigned to RT Crusader to be second in charge of the recon team. Sgt. Dale Dehnke was the 01 and had been at CCN for his third tour.

They had seven Montagard (Bru) mercenary' young men that had been fighting this war for many years and were fearless, strong physically and extremely combat experienced soldiers that could and did take care of them when it came to crises time.

He and Dale shared a hooch (sleeping quarters) that was a one room bunker. Da Nang did not receive mortar rounds and was secure, except every occasionally, a local individual would attempt to shoot or blow something up based on the theory of civilians by day and guerrillas by night. The Green Beret's would launch their recon missions from either the compound at Marble Mountain north of Da Nang or the air base in Da Nang, Northern Thailand or from Quan Tri.

There were about forty other teams with about 80 to a hundred Americans in the compound. The missions varied from a point recon (identify a specific target) and destroy by air strikes. There was always an attempt to capture some important NVA military person, to recovering downed Air Force pilots in Laos and southern North Viet Nam. During his time, he told me all the teams could not wait to go out and retrieve a live downed pilot on a recovery mission. That did happen in their camp. Most the pilots however would attempt to reach the sea area if possible. There were a lot of air force prisoners of war, since all most all of them either died in the plane crash. If they did parachute out they were usually deep into enemy territory and it was difficult to get to them quick enough prior to their capture.

RT Crusader went on three missions with Dale as the 01 and my brother as the 1-1. On the second mission they went into Laos for a point recon of a large NVA unit. They inserted by helicopter by riding on the struts and then jumping off onto the ground. There were six of them total and they intended to spend four days sneaking around attempting to pinpoint this unit. The weather turned bad and it rained the entire eleven days. They could not get extracted as planned because it was socked in with low clouds and fogged in. They got a radio message that the NVA had witnessed their insertion and were on the hunt for them. They moved the first four days several miles, which is very risky and hard to do in the jungle. At one time they were close enough to the NVA camp to see that they were sending out patrols looking for them.

He counted about twenty-five of them one time about forty feet away. They had no food after the 7th day, but lots of water since it was raining. The weather lifted the morning of the eleventh day and headquarters launched an extraction mission. They were forced to once again move about ½ mile away, picked a LZ (landing zone for helicopters) and late that morning the choppers came in beneath the clouds and fog.

The team was extracted by hooking onto ladders (with snap links) that were dropped from the choppers and hung there beneath the helicopter on the ladders until they reached a Marine outpost called Khe Son which was on top of a mountain.

Totally exhausted and with hypothermia from being wet and hanging beneath the helicopter for over thirty minutes, they all just unhooked and laid there until the medics got then going again. Steve ended up in the hospital for three days and had Emersion Foot (skin peeled off his feet) because they were wet, and he had not taken his boots off for eleven days. He still to this day has issues with his feet, as they are still real sensitive and sweat easily.

When they went into the field everyone took minimum food, communication equipment (the best the Army had), AR-15 (altered M-16), and about eight clips of twenty rounds each and three to four small hand grenades. The packs were about thirty to forty pounds. No one was ever overweight!!

Steve's last mission with Dale was right after they had trained RT Crusader to jump by parachute out of a C-123 off the rear supply ramp. They practiced five times and just a few days later an American jet was shot down near the Cambodian border and the pilots ejected out and had been captured. They were being moved north to North Viet Nam prison camps. At least that was what the intelligence whether it was good or bad.

Headquarters decided quickly, since RT Crusader's team was trained and ready they designed a quick mission to attempt to insert by parachute and snatch the pilots from the NVA moving the captured pilot's north.

RT Crusader jumped off the tail gate of the C-123 jumped at 1:00 AM. The sky was clear and calm, but there was a fog bank on the deck. Steve remembered the plane was eight-hundred feet above the jungle canopy. Eight-hundred feet off the ground is at under the best of circumstances not good. They had practiced hooking the canopy of the parachute into the top of the tree canopy and then hook up a rappelling rope to the canopy harness and rappel down to the ground. They were carrying hundred foot ropes and the jungle canopy was about one-hundred and twenty-five ft., so they all had a serious problem. Steve dropped off the end of the rope and crashed hard and knocked himself unconscious. One Bru (Bru is a Montgand tribe name) fell off the end of the rope and broke both of his femur bones above the knees.

Another Bru attempted to climb back up the rope and became wrapped up with a half hitch knot around his left arm. Dale and one other Bru got on the ground without getting hurt. There were all messed up with no chance to continue the mission and high odds of being killed or captured. Just imagine how hard it is to get together in total darkness under a jungle canopy with three people hurt or out cold.

At daylight Dale got everyone organized and called to abort the mission and again the extraction team was there immediately. The Bru with the broken legs did not make it to the hospital and died. The Bru with the left arm ½ hitch was paralyzed in his arm. Steve spent about a week in the hospital with bumps and bruises. The Red Cross called home and he had the pleasure to tell our mother that he had fallen out of a tree. Not one shot was fired in either of the above mission reports, but as you can tell high risk missions create opportunity to get in trouble or get hurt seriously.

Steve went to Headquarters in Da Nang to be promoted to sergeant. Dale boot strapped and went on a special mission with RT Anaconda. Steve was flying back to the compound and was listing to a radio frequency band and heard Lt. Danny Entricon the 01 of RT Alaska. They had just got ambushed by small arms fire on a ridge and Dale the 03 and Sgt Hollingsworth the 02 were both dead and the team had scattered into the jungle. His voice was broken and quiet as he knew he was in real trouble. The pilot lost contact with him before they landed at the compound. CCN command had already launched a strike team to attempt to help or at least recover whom they could. They found both bodies of the 02 and 03 and one Montagard. Lt. Entricon was not there or anywhere nearby. He is still listed as MIA (missing in action). All three are listed on the Viet Nam Memorial in Washington DC.

Several days later several of the team had escaped and crossed back into friendly territory and got back to the compound. This was the worst and most serious blow to my brother during the entire war. Dale and he had become friends and were living, playing, training and running recon together. They were both independent and confident of what we were doing.

Dale chose to go back one too many times and he ran out of luck. There is another chapter to Dale's death. At the time of his death, Dale's parents were in a bitter divorce. His father had sent him titles to two Bell helicopters which Steve witnessed Dale signing over to his father and his father had signed them over to Dale. This was done just in case one or the other was killed. They each were worth approx. $500,000.

The divorce settlement was over the value of these helicopters. Dale's father was also upset because the Army sent his body to the ex-wife for burial instead of him. He also thought that Dale should at least receive the Silver Star

Medal.

Upon Steve's return to the States he went to go see Dale's father and give him a sense of how he was killed. Steve's close friend Mark Farstvedt went with him to Van Nuys California to see him. He was upset about the funeral arrangements, lack of info on how he was killed, and no recognition for bravery. Dale's father committed suicide several months later as he sat on his son's grave. Steve had to go to Van Nuys to testify in court about the signatures on the pick slips. He still gets upset that this issue dragged on several years after he returned. The helicopters became more important than the death of a great friend!

Steve took over RT Crusader after Sgt. Dale Dehnke's death and ran one more mission into the DMZ. He remembers being in the DMZ and things were not going well (hard to move without being detected). He decided to abort and called for extraction. They took small arms fire as they were beneath the chopper on the ladders. He could hear the rounds hitting the chopper and fortunately the Huey keep flying and no one on the ladders got wounded.

Steve flew covey pilot for his final six weeks in country. After one had some ground experience the covey pilot assignment was a perk as there was way less risk. They could talk the language for insertions, extractions and to place air support. Knowing this language became very critical when contact (a fire fight) with the enemy was made either by accident or intentionally. The covey pilot's job was to assess and decide when and how to extract or obtain additional support. All teams when inserted always had an OV-10 or OV-6 above them twenty-four hours a day.

This was a fun part of the overall experience as he got to see the country from the air and ride with some very gutsy air force pilots. The only real scare was one day as they returned to the ground the pilot got out of the plane and showed him a bullet hole in the right propeller. Several occasions in Laos they shot at his plane with Sam missiles.

The country side was very much like the Oregon Coast Range and the Willamette Valley if it were semi-flooded. A lot of country-side was burned and pocked marked with bomb craters. He never had much interaction with the people of Viet Nam. They were just too busy moving around and planning for what they did. For each mission all teams usually spent at least one weeks training for that mission and gathering intelligence about the surrounding area and if there were any enemy present.

Their compound was first class with a real restaurant and lounge. They also got a big perk for doing these missions which was several days off. He ended up in Thailand twice. He received the Bronze Star, Arcom with Valor, Vietnamese Jump Wings, and the Combat Infantry Badge.

He was never disappointed that he volunteered to go to Viet Nam. He said he grew up real fast and came home with a lot of confidence that has help him in other parts of his life including a very viable and successful real estate career. He has never really struggled with the stress issues some other veterans had to. The only cause and affect has been his sleeping habits have always been poor.

Yes, like all of us combat veterans he does jump or flinch when a noise is unexpected. Or one someone sneaks up behind him. In his later years he also has a habit of reviewing his experiences in Viet Nam. He tends to rehash or regurgitate those experiences internally. This is much like dreams or day dreaming. We all do, those of us who were there. He gives a lot of thanks to the Man above and, his wife, and other supporters that helped him be injury free.

Recently he was diagnosed with Lymphoma Cancer. The Veteran's Administration has determined that this cancer likely came from Agent Orange and therefore has classified him as 100% Service Disabled.

There was a quote in the CCN compound that stated: "YOU HAVE NEVER LIVED UNTIL YOU HAVE ALMOST DIED, SOMETHING A RECON MAN ONLY KNOWS!!"

My brother Steve has always been good to me. He was always there when I needed him. Supported me through all my trials and challenges Vietnam related or not. He never gave up on me from my alcohol addiction. For this I thank him and will always be there for him.

EPILOGUE

Much has happened in my life since Vietnam. Fifty plus years seems like a long time. It really isn't in the context of time. Some of the experiences I have shared with you seem like yesterday. There are a lot more I could write about but choose not to. I see no reason to share those kinds and types of war experiences.

I am just one ordinary soldier fortunate to have made it this long in life. I feel grateful that I have my health and a still-clear frame of mind, allowing me to tell the story of those twenty-six impressionable months in my life.

The debate is still going on if I am crazy or not among those that have known me that are still alive. Most of those involved in that debate for years have passed on.

My experiences in Vietnam are constantly on my mind and have shaped my life as it is today.

Every day there, shaped the rest of my life in ways that are hard even for me to grasp. The effect of some of those experiences has been negative; that I admit and recognize most of what was good and what was bad. Yet the time I was so fortunate to spend with General Rosson had an immensely positive everlasting influence on my sense of character and the man I have aspired to be.

Perhaps my children and a few others who know me read this will now have some insight as to why I behaved the way I did at times—why I thought about things the way I did and still do. Why things at times weren't so easy for me. We all react differently, process things differently and re-member things differently.

A lot of guys had it a lot tougher than I did.

ABOUT THE AUTHOR

DAVID AND DEBORAH SCOTT

DAVID H. SCOTT served in Vietnam from October 1966 to October 1968. Extending two different tours for a total of three tours of duty for a total of twenty-six months. He spent his 19th, 21st and 22nd birthdays in Vietnam. His first twelve-month tour of duty was as an Infantry Soldier in combat with the B-2 502 101st Airborne. His 1st extension was for six months to be Lt. General Rosson's personal driver. The second six month extension was as his driver and then became Lt. General Rosson's personal enlisted aide. Upon Lt. General Rosson's rotation from Vietnam, Mr. Scott became Lt. General Stilwell's personal enlisted aide until he finally went home for good.

After the war Mr. Scott worked construction and owned businesses. A fireplace shop, a painting business in Anchorage, Alaska, several construction companies, a Service Disabled Veteran Owned Small Business, superintended projects, a motel and RV Park, an energy conservation retrofit lighting business, mortgage loan officer, sold real estate, was a Mayor of a small Eastern Oregon community.

Mr. Scott married in his mid-twenties, had five children two boys and three girls. The first boy Brad drowned in an irrigation ditch in Bend, Oregon at the age of sixteen months. Cameron, Angie, Chrissi and Lavonne are all healthy, active and successful young adults. The first marriage ended in divorce after 8 years and he remarried Deborah at the age of 40.

Mr. Scott is a 100% Service Disabled Veteran.

He has been clean and sober as of September 1, 2017 for twenty years after getting nine DUI's over a period of twenty-seven years. Something he is not proud of, but he is grateful for his sobriety and finally figuring out how to be an adult and live a full life.

Mr. Scott is an avid solo kayaker, kayaking long trips. He also river rafts extensively.

In 2014, he kayaked/river rafted the Snake River in the Western United States from Flagg Ranch, Wyoming to the Columbia River in Washington a total of 1,200 miles, forty-two days.

In 2016, he kayaked the Yellowstone River, starting at Gardiner, Montana, to the Missouri River west of Williston, North Dakota, to the Mississippi at St. Louis, Illinois then on down to Baton Rouge, Louisiana. Close to 3,000 miles, one-hundred days.

In 2017, he kayaked the Yukon River, leaving White-horse, Yukon and ended his trip prematurely at the Native Village of Grayling, Alaska because his thumbs and his thumb joints gave out on him. A total of 1,600 miles, fif-ty-five days with less than two hundred and fifty miles to go.

He is also the author of:

101 Ways to Tell the World to Kiss Your Ass.

Mr. Scott's website is

www.1indsob.com

One can communicate with him on the contact tab in the website.